TAROT CARDS:
A READER'S WORKBOOK

Tarot Cards:
A Reader's Workbook

By Qumran Taj

Crown Prince Publications

www.qumrantaj.com

About the Author

Qumran Taj has led a life that can only be described as a rather 'mixed bag.' For many years he was a well respected Christian minister, public speaker and teacher. In time his view of religion, spirituality and the unseen spirit realms led him to explore well beyond the boundaries of Church dogma. Simultaneously Qumran, or "Q" as he is called by family and friends, began to cultivate the spiritual gifts he had neglected since early childhood. Psychic gifts or 'gifts of the Spirit' had always manifested in his life, as early as six years old, but his Church frowned on such abilities so they went largely ignored until much later in life. Eventually, Q's true calling became clear. He is now known far and wide as "The Wizard," a wise teacher and counselor, who is a recognized authority on Witchcraft, Wicca, magick, Tarot, psychic and paranormal phenomena. Q is the author of *"Tarot Cards: A Reader's Workbook"* and *"The Hidden Forest"* in addition to various poems and short stories. *He is the creator of numerous classes, courses and seminars such as Transform Your Life With Practical Magick, 13 Moons of Wizardry and The Imaginal Realm.* Q has been quoted by or had his articles published in respected publications such as *New York Magazine, Newsday, Creations Magazine, Long Island Press, The Village,* and others. He has been interviewed for TV and feature films. He currently writes, lectures, teaches and does intuitive counseling and coaching for groups and individuals. Q lives with his family on Long Island, New York. For more information visit: www.qumrantaj.com

©2013 by Qumran Taj. All rights reserved.

This book contains material protected under International and Federal Copyright Laws and Treaties. Any unauthorized reprint or use of this material is prohibited. No part of this book may be reproduced or transmitted in any form or by any means, electronic or mechanical, including photocopying, recording, or by any information storage and retrieval system without express written permission from the author or Crown Prince Publications.

Picture credits:

Cover photo (center color) and Tarot spreads photography by Christina Maury.

The cards used in spreads pictured are the "Wizards Tarot" by John Blumen.

All other photos and clip art are either in the public domain or royalty and copyright free.

Proudly printed and bound in the United State of America.

ISBN-13: 978-0615926018 (Crown Prince Publications)
ISBN-10: 0615926010

Dedicated with all my heart to:

my mom.

Your genius was love.

Acknowledgments

Does a name or scant crediting phrase really do justice to the contributions those special individuals make to one's project? How would this book have been different minus the generous help, kind corrections and thinly veiled rolling eyes of the following people? I cannot say. What I *can* say is that I am deeply grateful for all their efforts to make me look good in spite of myself!

I owe my humble gratitude to:

Cathy Maury for editorial assistance, her analytical mind and unfailing support for everything I do.

Christina Maury for her photographic expertise.

Undeniably, a man is shaped by all the souls he meets in life. Their mark is made somehow, somewhere but it is not always apparent to the casual observer. To all who have 'marked' me for better or worse, I give heartfelt thanks. You have all made me who I am today.

Table of Contents:

Acknowledgments

		page:
Chapter 1:	Of Tarot Cards, Mystery and Magick	11
Chapter 2:	The "Right" vs The "Wrong" Way to Read	22
Chapter 3:	Choosing Your First Deck	32
Chapter 4:	The Versatile Tarot	41
Chapter 5:	Anatomy of a Tarot Deck	51
Chapter 6:	Worksheets	65
Chapter 7:	Spreads to Suit Your Needs	78
Chapter 8:	Symbols and Correspondences	93
Chapter 9:	Numbers and What They Mean	100
Chapter 10:	So Now What?	104
Chapter 11:	The End … or The Beginning?	111

Chapter 1

Of Tarot Cards, Mystery and Magick

§

Chloe, Randy and Gwen huddled before the ancient oak door. They stood transfixed, as though the door handle was a deadly cobra, fangs bared and poised to strike a death blow. Randy reminded himself this was only an old storefront, albeit one that made his stomach knot. His 'crew,' two girls bubbling over with nervous giggles, glanced back and forth down the street. It simply wouldn't do for someone to spy them entering the crazy Witchcraft shoppe. That uncomfortable possibility gave Randy the extra shot of courage he needed to yank the snake's head and open the forbidden portal. Like some mutated 6 legged, 6 armed humanoid, the three jumpy-bumpy baby-stepped through the door as a single unit. Once through, smoky tendrils embraced each in turn and the rich scent of incense began a journey they would never forget. At once there were a thousand things to see. Strange things. Too much to take in at once, so Gwen, with her long, glossy pigtails and rainbow colored wool cap, reminded them that their mission was to get a Tarot card reading and report what it was like to the outside world.

§

Stray into the New Age or Occult aisles of your favorite bookstore and you will find Tarot decks and books that explain them. Tarot cards and "readings" are more popular with each passing year. During difficult and uncertain times many people consult the cards in search of insight and guidance. While it is unwise to rely solely on the Tarot to make life's most important decisions, there is value in learning how to read them. In my psychic and spiritual counseling practice I have often been amazed at how the cards seem to have a story to tell. If you allow your mind and intuition to decipher the messages contained in the card "spreads" you might be amazed as well.

The origin of these cards is mysterious. Mythologies and misinformation abound. Experts disagree on the particulars. This uncertainty has given the more creative among us a golden opportunity to conjure all kinds of titillating theories. The most notable of these was the Frenchman *Antoine Court, or Antoine Court de Gébelin* as he preferred. In 1773, he fabricates an imaginative "history" of the Tarot. In his landmark essay *Le Monde primitif, analysé et comparé avec le monde moderne,* in the small section on Tarot he weaves a tale wherein the cards originate in ancient Egypt.

According to Gébelin the Egyption god Thoth imparted his mystical wisdom to priests and sorcerers via its images. Not surprisingly his exotic ideas were embraced far and wide and became accepted as historical truth-despite the absence of facts or evidence as best we can tell. Other stories have the Hebrew Moses consulting the Tarot. Even King Solomon of Biblical lore is said to have used the Tarot to establish his reputation as the wisest man of his time.

So what do we really know of these often misunderstood tools of divination? Let us first understand that the journey of the Tarot is an epic adventure spanning eight centuries. Virtually every country around the globe contributed to this saga. In other words, many things were happening in many places simultaneously over a very, very long time. The history isn't crystal clear. Even the dates cited below are open to some debate, although, they are close enough to give an accurate picture overall. A truly comprehensive history of the cards would require several encyclopedic volumes to relate. Telling that story is far beyond the scope and intent of this workbook. The following time line is widely accepted as factual history.

Tarot de Marseille (1760) c.1870 edition shown here from original woodblocks and screened color.

800's	Hand painted playing cards invented in China about same time as paper began being used for pages instead of long scrolls.
1000's	Playing cards have spread to all of Asia and often feature images of fictional characters. They're also used as trading cards, game currency or "money cards."
1377	Playing cards have entered Europe, probably from Egypt. Suits are polo sticks, coins, swords, cups. Abstract images are used in conjunction with religious icons and notable characters from fiction and history.

1411–1430	First Tarot decks invented in Italy. Originally the cards were called 'Trionfi,' "Tarot" being a mispronunciation of 'Tarocchi' or 'Tarock'-the name of the game played with the cards. For the first time archetypal "trump" cards are added to the standard playing deck.
1540	*Francesco Marcolini* publishes the first book on *Cartomancy*, or divination using cards. It should be noted, however, that his book focused on using ordinary playing cards, not primarily the Tarot. Also, remember that Cartomancy had been used long before books had been published about it.
1500's	Tarot decks proliferate along with rule books for playing games with them.
1730–1830	Modern Tarot decks develop in northern Italy, eastern France, Switzerland, Germany, Belgium, the Netherlands, Denmark, Sweden, Russia and elsewhere.
1773	*Antoine Court de Gébelin* authors his famous essay *Le Monde primitif, analysé et comparé avec le monde moderne*. His ideas are widely accepted.
1770–	"Etteilla," aka *Jean-Baptiste Alliette*, popularized

1785	Tarot cards for occult uses. He publishes his thoughts on card meanings and describes specific methods and techniques for "reading" them.
1800's	Tarot experiences a 'reinvention.' Symbolism and correspondences are redefined, changed and replaced by other elements, adding to the Tarot folklore. These changes make the cards better suited for divination, fortunetelling and other occult uses.
1910	The famous *Rider-Waite-Smith Tarot deck* is published by *Arthur Edward Waite* and illustrator *Pamela Colman Smith*.
1911	*The Pictorial Key to the Tarot* is published by *Arthur Edward Waite* (an expanded version of his book *The Key to the Tarot*.)
1900's	The advent of the computer age, and no little thanks to internet search engines like Google, makes Tarot available to billions of individuals with a few computer keystrokes. Many significant contributors to Tarot history could be named here but space does not permit. Interest in the Tarot skyrockets in the 20th century.

Since the first hand painted cards appeared in the 14th century and later evolved into our modern traditional deck, literally thousands of new and fantastic designs have appeared. Themes feature everything from super heroes to dogs and cats, fairies, vampires, angels, unicorns, dragons, witches and many more! There is a theme for nearly every interest. The important thing to remember is that the meanings for individual cards are by no means standardized but they tend to have fairly consistent similarities. Having said that, the diversification of symbolism and themes are also gradually changing the messages of the cards. In my humble opinion, the changes we see in the iconography and interpretation of the individual cards is inevitable and part of the healthy, normal evolution of this tool. Lest someone imagine I'm suggesting the cards are somehow losing their value to the modern reader, allow me to make one point perfectly clear. As long as the cards continue to represent the stages and experience of the human condition, both positive and negative, Tarot will always be relevant.

Magick

The Use of Tarot cards in magick is a natural progression from divination. One is an effort to see the future and the other is an effort to influence it. The theory of magick says that everything is connected in ways that are unseen yet very real. The connection is an energetic one. Since science agrees that everything is composed of energy it follows that everything that happens in this world is a result of one form of energy interacting with another form. It is a rather simple concept. You reach out your hand to pick up a glass of your favorite beverage. Your hand appears solid enough. The glass waits patiently for you to move it and the beverage stays obediently in its glass container until something changes that fact.

Despite appearances to the contrary, your hand is NOT solid but rather is made of untold trillions of sub-atomic particles vibrating at near the speed of light. In fact, things that are small enough or vibrate at a high enough frequency can pass through your arm as if it weren't even there. The same holds true of the "solid" glass and the liquid inside it. In actual truth nothing at all is solid. It is also equally true that you have never actually touched another solid object with your hand or any other part of your body for that matter. The reason for this is that there is an energy threshold or barrier, if you will, created by the atomic energy or electrons that make up all so-called material objects. This energy literally repels anything you come into contact with. It also repels your own touch. Naturally, this atomic barrier is infinitesimally thin and impossible to see but it is, nevertheless, there. Occasionally we do well to remind ourselves that superficial appearances are not usually an accurate representation of reality. This discussion of magick aside, any scientist will confirm that everything that appears 'solid' and stationary is neither. In truth, EVERYTHING you perceive in your environment is actually moving at incredible speeds. NOTHING is ever standing still. Furthermore, spaces between solid objects may appear empty but they most certainly are not. Energy fills the spaces in between everything everywhere. The fundamental theory behind magick is that everything everywhere is connected by energy and can be accessed and affected from any other place regardless of distance. Although scientists are loath to relent on this point, it is difficult to ignore that there is a scientific basis for belief in a magickal reality. It might help us to grasp the concept by imagining a kind of spiritual 'internet.' In this analogy every person is a computer terminal capable of searching out information from anywhere or anyone else. Take a moment to think of the possibilities!

So where do the cards come into this picture? The cards, being part of our universe, are also connected. When the mind is focused on a particular question or magickal intention, the cards "react" and potentially reflect relevant information. This cannot be proven scientificly. Nevertheless, the results of so-called magickal activity, subjective though they may be, are intriguing. There DOES appear to be a correlation between powerful, focused intention, the Tarot and results achieved. Let us not forget that Tarot cards were not originally designed with magick in mind. In actual fact, any picture can be used as a visual aid in focusing the mind to a given purpose. The Tarot is not exclusively a tool of magick but it can be put to that service in the same way one might use a seashell as a censer to burn incense during ritual. Grandma's ring was not created for magick but it can certainly be used for that purpose if you know how. Contrary to popular opinion, magick is not a supernatural phenomenon at all. More accurately, the energies used are quite natural although not commonly known or understood. It is "supernatural" only insofar as scientists have not yet acknowledged it as part of the natural scheme of things. Let us be careful, however, not to use too broad a brush in painting scientists as a group. To be fair, there is a pretty substantial number of very highly respected theoretical and quantum physicists that have made truly epic discoveries with far-reaching ramifications. This new science (old science really, but newly discovered) speaks to the existence of other dimensions, parallel universes, the nature of time itself and many, many other topics that have a direct correlation to what I would call magickal truth. As I have said many times before it is the scientists, in my humble opinion, that will eventually uncover the *who, why, where, how and when* of psychic phenomena, magick, and a multitude of other unexplained happenings. When science finally figures all of this out I suspect they will not call it magick anymore. It will then be repackaged and re-labeled in a way more to their liking. Will this be the end of magick in the world? I think not. Still. the jargon will doubtless change and it will all become common knowledge. One can only hope!

"The Whole World in His Hands" by Qumran Taj

Chapter 2

The "Right" vs The "Wrong" Way to Read

☙☢

The floors were old, creaky and pitted. Chloe's eyes roller-coasted around in her head in an effort to take in her surroundings as quickly as possible. What she saw revved up her imagination in ways that made her rethink if this little adventure was a good idea after all. In display cases of dark woods worn blond by the touch of countless fingers anxiously caressing its edges, Chloe saw pointy daggers with odd handles made of deer antlers, wire, leather, jewels and crystals. There were statues of horned men or gods, half man half goat, Egyptian deities, crosses and crucifixes, pentacles and pentagrams, beautiful figurines of regal ladies, Celtic knot-work and runes on rings and pendants and even ornate swords! There were turkey feathers dyed in bright primary colors, candles in the shapes of man and woman, skulls, the Horned God, pyramids and more. Gwen admired a clothes rack heavy with long flowing robes, cloaks and other garments made in luxurious colors, velvet, cotton, wool and even leather. The atmosphere of the place was dramatic with small track lights casting brilliant circles on exotic jewels and pretentious chalices fit for kings and queens. The electric glint of steel, semi-precious stones and crystal candlestick holders contrasted with the gentle glow of ubiquitous candles standing as flaming sentinels in every quarter of this magickal shoppe.

Randy pried himself away from the girls. He took a few cautious steps toward the interior of this strange place. There were book shelves but the titles were curious and unfamiliar to him. Spirit guides, Astral Travel– whatever that was–Wicca, Druids, fairies, gods and goddesses galore! There was the curious absence of customers and the shoppe keep was nowhere to be seen. Tom walked down an aisle with shelves of dusty old jars with handwritten labels. Plants were inside those jars but they looked so very dry, as though life had left them years ago. Horehound, Mandrake Root, Damiana, Sage, Devil's Shoestring and Burdock Root. There were so many.

Gwen's reaction was different than the rest. She saw little she had ever seen before and even less she understood. Even so, she wanted to learn more. Somehow she sensed this was a world that was connected to her in a way she could scarcely explain. All she really knew was that she felt at home here. How odd! It was like she had been here before in a dream. She got that feeling when you become aware that someone is watching you. She looked all around but still saw no one. Her feet led her. No, the dream led her. Nothing made sense but it was what needed to happen. Five minutes passed. Maybe more. Who could know for sure? Randy and Chloe began to wonder why they were standing in a store that was open for business and yet they appeared to be the only people around! Weird! And, by the way, where was Gwen?

☙❦

Before we move on we should address the question that traditionalists will undoubtedly raise. Isn't there a "right" way to interpret the cards? Do not the symbolic images have a specific meaning? Isn't there a wrong way to interpret the oracle? I would answer that this depends. The person doing the interpreting is a key factor here. Since every individual is just that – an individual- it strikes me as being either terribly arbitrary or insufferably arrogant to be inflexible on this point. Consider the following example. In the Thoth deck, which I use in my own readings, the Emperor has bumble bees on his royal vestments. We may have learned in our studies that bumble bees can symbolize joy, harmony, blessing and creativity. This same card also features Aries the ram, the *fleurdelis,* a double phoenix, the Maltese cross and the list goes on! Each symbol has a diverse range of possible meanings that may also vary from culture to culture. Can you imagine the almost unlimited number of possible interpretations there could be when these symbols are combined together on a single card?

Sure, there is usually a generic meaning assigned to the card as described in the book about that deck but oftentimes these meanings are either overly simplistic or so dreadfully esoteric they defy comprehension! They do not always tell you how all of the symbols have a bearing on the interpretation but instead leave you to simply recall the explanation by wrote. Furthermore, authors of any book cannot help but insert their own personal perspectives. Pick up enough books on Tarot and you'll discover that there are usually not-so-subtle differences in how each author characterizes each card. Which description is the "right" one? Do you go with what 'ABC book of Tarot' says or what 'A-Z Tarot Book' says? Assuming the authors haven't plagiarized each other the descriptions will be different. One cannot escape getting a different shade of meaning from each writer. Now consider that there are thousands of books about the Tarot written by thousands of opinionated authors. Let us add to this lovely mix the fact that different decks may use imagery for the Emperor card that is entirely different than the ones I described! To traditionalist who insist on rigid, conventional meanings of the cards I say, *suit yourself!* My students will always be given the option to follow whatever methods that seem to work best for them.

After all, the iconic symbols on most Tarot sets did not come down from heaven inscribed on stone tablets by the finger of God. They *evolved* over the course of many centuries. So many people, places and cultures contributed to our modern forms that even scholars have a hard time tracking them! Not to put too fine a point on it, while there is certainly much wisdom distilled into our modern deck, the intuitive leading of Spirit should always trump the writings of authors long dead. Is not the objective of any reading to benefit from it? It follows then that if you achieve your objective it matters little if you used conventional or unconventional means. When in doubt, follow your gut. You would be amazed at how accurate readings can be when you listen to that 'quiet voice' inside. Finally, for a beginner I recommend choosing one deck and one book and sticking with it for a while. As time goes on and you become more seasoned and comfortable with the basics by all means branch out. Obtain other decks, other books and read everything you can get your hands on.

Given what we just considered in the section on magick and the interconnectedness of all things, it stands to reason that almost *anything* could be used as an oracle or a magickal device provided the "rules" have been decided upon or ascertained before you start asking questions of it. Intuitive people who consult other types of oracles such as tea leaves, the flight of birds, animal tracks or even patterns on charred bones, for example, will be able to read them to some advantage provided the 'ground rules' are clear. As I stated before, this cannot be proven scientificly. It is nonetheless true. You may choose to decide for yourself that all of this simply makes no logical sense at all and trash the whole concept, or you can decide that there are limits to scientific knowledge and read on. Allow me to assure you that I am not telling stories to tickle your ears. I know wherefore I speak, my friend.

By now you realize that I am not the biggest fan of rigid structures and inflexible interpretations when it comes to Tarot reading. So it may puzzle my good readers that I refer to the rules of this art. Understand that the "rules" I speak of do not necessarily have to come from books or teachers. That is to say, 'how to' books or instructors are not absolutely necessary to learn to read oracles. Nevertheless, experience has taught me that some people prefer structured, precise instructions so that they will know the "right" way to do things. These people feel more comfortable if there is a step-by-step procedure laid out by some authority on the subject. If this sounds a little like you, rest assured, it is a perfectly fine way to proceed. The instructions in this book will satisfy that need. Do not forget, however, that there is a large part of card reading that depends on developing your intuition. For this reason book learning must go hand in hand with intuitive inspiration. Intuition cannot be learned like an academic subject. Herein lies the challenge for pure book learners. Not to worry, though. Every time you pick up your deck it is another opportunity for you to test and sharpen your interpretive skills.

It may seem strange to say it in this context but, when I was a young boy I used to love reading comic books. They are laid out in graphic panels across the page. Each panel will have an illustration and sometimes dialog. In this graphic novel format you follow the story by seeing the collective panels as a whole and not standing alone. The Tarot cards should be read in like manner. It is best when you train your mind to interpret the spread as a story told in pictures with each individual card like a comic book panel. Each card is part of a larger narrative. Each individual card comments on a particular point of interest in said narrative. This feature of the overall picture has particular importance to the querant (the person you're reading for) and it should be addressed for them.

What will be your policy on so-called "reverse" or "inverse" meanings? When a card is selected and laid on the table upside down some people interpret this as having a "reverse" or "inverse" meaning. In this context "reverse" means negative. For instance, the 'Wheel of Fortune' upside down would likely be read as an omen of *bad* fortune. Personally, I prefer not to use "reverse" meanings. Speaking for myself alone, the question of positive or negative connotations are indicated by intuition and the relative position of a card to others in the spread. Readings can be just as accurate for someone using reverse meanings as not. The cards will "speak" to the reader in a way he or she can understand. The particular oracle used matters less than how you decide to use it and your connection with it. Surprisingly enough, even if your technical knowledge of the cards and symbolism is very limited, the messages coming to you will be appropriate for your level of understanding. That is why you should decide for yourself what standard procedure seems most comfortable for you and stick with that.

Much is written about the many kinds of "spreads" you can use. A spread is the pattern you lay the cards out in on the table. Each position in the spread pattern has its own unique focus. Some are laid out like a pentagram, a crown, a cross or even a crescent moon. There are a variety of spreads illustrated later on in this book. They definitely have their use and some are particularly well suited to certain kinds of questions. You will probably want to experiment with them and even memorize a few. Maybe the best known of the Tarot card spreads is the "Celtic Cross." This is a whole life spreads that speaks to career, love, family, personal challenges, etc. It is a very popular spread. Try it and see if it 'fits' you well. If you want to use some other card pattern, by all means try it out!

Antoine Court de Gébelin (b. ca. 1719 d. 1784) wrote his famous essay, *Le Monde primitif, analysé et comparé avec le monde moderne* in 1781. Only one small section addressed his theories on the Tarot but his ideas transformed Tarot forever. He fabricated a "history" of the cards that became widely accepted as fact despite the total lack of evidence.

Chapter 3

Choosing Your First Deck

※

Three long aisles ran from the front to the rear of the store. Chloe and Randy each took an outside aisle and started toward the rear of this large deserted room. One thing became clear; Gwen was NOT in this room with them. Both kids were now convinced their worst fears were about to come true. This was a BAD idea! They forced their legs to carry them deeper into the store when all they wanted to do was run away. Snakelike ropes of incense patrolled menacingly overhead. At the rear of the store there was a doorway that had been covered over completely with heavy drapes. The silence of this nightmare was broken by a queer chortle abruptly cut short. Randy and Chloe exchanged wide-eyed glances. Terror stricken eyes met for the briefest moment and communicated what they both knew in their hearts; that was NOT Gwen's voice. Both friends were frozen in place. A brief but fierce battle raged within each youngster. What can I do now? They so wanted to escape. Escape before it was too late! Despite the rising dread building in them they both knew they could never look themselves in the mirror if they abandoned Gwen in the bowels of this god forsaken place.

Chloe reached the curtain first. Just then a loud bell sounded by the front door! The kids were startled and all eyes turned to see two men enter. Chloe heard footsteps directly behind those drapes. Instinctively, she jumped to one side of the hidden doorway, just in time to avoid a large, portly woman who thrust past those heavy brocade drapes and stepped through. The lady knew the men and let shine a disarmingly friendly smile. "How are you boys today?" she began. This time it was Randy who leaped into action. As the rotund proprietor engaged herself with the new customers he and then Chloe slipped through the veil hiding the rear doorway.

૪⌘ↄ

For the beginner buying a deck is probably the first step on their journey but it can be a somewhat intimidating one. Since Tarot has become so popular these days the variety of decks available has grown exponentially. The forerunners of our modern cards began as hand painted works of art back in the fourteenth century but in our twenty first century they are now mass produced with pictures that feature hundreds of colors and truly breathtaking graphics. Many people collect them for their artistic value alone. You have access, either in stores or online, to hundreds if not THOUSANDS of different decks of every shape, size, theme and price point.

So how does one choose the right deck? I suggest you not spend much time worrying about it. You are not marrying the cards! In fact, most Tarot readers have several decks and go between them as the mood strikes or use one deck for reading and have the others for the pure joy the pictures give. Relax. Your first deck won't be your last. And let us not forget that you are on a journey of self-discovery. As with most quests, what you learn along the way is at least as valuable as arriving at the destination. If you have access to the internet it's an easy task to search Tarot decks and view sample pictures of each. If you're not a Google addict like me, visit any large bookstore chain.

The imagery that reaches out and grabs you deserves a closer look. This is one occasion when you want to give your intuition free reign. Reading the cards is largely an intuitive activity and so choose what feels right to you. Ultimately, the cards should please YOU. Simply looking at them should make you want to handle them, use them (even when you have no specific question for them!) In this regard no other opinion matters but yours. You like the cards? Buy them. End of discussion.

Cards vary widely in the images and artwork they contain.

Some artists make every element in the picture significant. The Thoth cards by Aliester Crowley and Lady Frieda Harris, for example, nearly overflow with symbolism from various cultures, Numerology and Astrology. The same could be said of the Hermetic deck or the Golden Dawn sets, of which there are many variations. Naturally, these warrant considerable study in order to get the most out of them. Having said that, even with decks that have complex layers of meaning and interpretation, never forget that they will "speak" to you based on whatever level of knowledge and understanding you possess *at the time you consult them.* That is to say, you can begin to use them with only a rudimentary understanding. As you learn more about your cards and gain experience using them, they will serve you better. You will become more attuned to the subtle messages contained in the symbols, colors and characters portrayed. Have fun with them! Avoid getting bogged down in the details and complexities of a spread. Make a habit of asking yourself, *"what do these cards say to ME?"* You may find this open-ended approach will make your readings more accurate and more valuable to all concerned.

It occurs to me that capitalistic impulses drive the proliferation of Tarot card styles and themes these days. I don't know what the sales statistics are but I've been around long enough to know that people spend lots of money on those 78 cards. Naturally, this makes dollar signs flash before the eyes of the more entrepreneurial souls among us. I have no issue with this because the end result is that there is a deck to fit almost every taste. There are even blank cards so you can make your own set.

What of those more fanciful themes, the Halloween Tarot, Homer Simpson or super hero decks? Are these too silly for the "serious" reader? In my opinion the answer is a resounding no! The magick of the cards is not in the pictures themselves but rather in your belief and approach to them. If you treat them with serious respect, they will perform as any others. The mere act of consulting them is what sets the divining process in motion. In my experience, the Universe is a responsive thing that reacts and responds to your thoughts and actions. When you ask the Universe for guidance it matters less the tool you use than your expectation that you will receive a reply.

Here is a cautionary note you will see repeated elsewhere in this book and it bears repeating. I do not recommend putting blind faith in *ANY* form of divination, including the Tarot. Why not? Firstly, the Tarot is not a substitute for using the brain God gave you to weigh all the facts available in order to make sound, rational choices. The cards may be used as a PART of your decision making process if you wish but not as a way to dodge responsibility for your decisions. Secondly, your interpretation of the cards may be skewed either through ignorance or personal bias. There is always a danger we will see what we *want* to see. I have been as guilty as the next person of casting a spread and deciding to engage in what you might call *'creative interpretation.'* You may not consciously, intentionally skew the reading but we are human beings after all, right? Take it from me. It really is hard *not* to see the cards confirming your heart's desire. Are me and my beloved going to grow old together and live happily ever after? What is that you say cards? Yes you say? YES!!? *I knew it!* Don't get the wrong idea, readers. I am not suggesting you shouldn't read your own cards. Quite to the contrary, I suggest you do many self-readings. Simply be aware that if you have a strong emotional bias or a vested interest in a certain outcome it could affect your perception. I still do my own cards but always take the results with a 'grain of salt' as they say!

To you beginners I say this: handle your cards! Get the *feel* of them. Get the *smell* of them. Shuffle them. Spend 'quality time' getting to know them in intimate detail. Pore over each and every card looking at the illustrations. Search for symbols, even hidden ones. Some decks use colors symbolically. Research the inner meaning. *Feel* their spirit and energy. A superior deck will reveal that its makers put an abundance of thought into their design. Explore. Climb into the scene and try to experience the reality of it. Some people believe the cards are alive. As a beginner I think I would have scoffed at such a notion. Having used them for so long I'm not so sure they aren't!

When I got my first deck I took a notebook and wrote my own impressions for all 78 cards. My thought was that I wanted to see what each card meant to me. What did they convey on a deep, visceral level? Now, mind you, I also took the time to read the book meaning for each card, carefully underlining salient points and making notes in the margins. Armed with what the cards were "supposed" to mean, I explored further to discover what they meant to me personally. For me this was a good thing since I didn't have to worry about forgetting the book definition of a card in the middle of a reading. It also eliminated the need to carry the book with me everywhere. The net result was that I was comfortable using both the book descriptions and the deeper meanings my inner sight saw in them.

Allow me to offer a suggestion regarding the handling and storage of your Tarot set. It should be treated with a degree of respect and stored in a secure, dignified place. After all, why would you consult anything or anyone you did not respect or care for? Some people suggest wrapping them in white satin or silk, others in black satin or velveteen. Suit yourself on this point but regardless of how you store them they should be safe from dampness, rough treatment, dust and dirt. Furthermore, although I wouldn't get paranoid about it, the truth is that they should be handled mostly by YOU. If you are reading another individual it is a fairly common practice to allow the querant the opportunity to shuffle the cards at some point. Allowing this practice is entirely up to you. A good reading can be effected either way but some readers (myself included) prefer to have the client shuffle the cards. After the reading is done many books recommend cleansing the deck of the vibrations and unique energy of your previous client. Once again, this is largely a matter of personal preference and your own belief system. It can't hurt to do a simple cleansing ritual if you have any concerns about residual negative energies from your last session. Some ideas for a quickie cleansing are passing the deck through the smoke of sage, frankincense and myrrh or place a quartz crystal atop the stack. Leaving it in the cleansing sunlight for a bit or simply saying a Prayer will also do nicely.

Pamela Colman Smith (b.1878-d.1951,) nicknamed "Pixie," was an author and illustrator. Perhaps her most famous work was illustrating the famous Rider-Waite-Smith Tarot deck. Smith also illustrated books for such notables as Bram Stoker and William Butler Yeats. An author/illustrator of several of her own books Smith also published a magazine called *The Green Sheaf* and contributed her artwork in support of woman's suffrage in Great Britain.

Chapter 4

The Versatile Tarot

ಸುಂಡ

They entered what looked like an old time kitchen with a little ancient dinette that had been stuck in time since the 1950's. It was your typical Formica table top with chrome metal legs and chairs upholstered in vinyl, sporting matching chrome legs, complete with a chair handle on top. To the right was another doorway (no door) into a room that seemed to be lit entirely by candles. On the left a door was set beside a hallway that was, at least partially, lit by sunlight. Neither youth could see where the hallway led from their vantage point.

Randy and Chloe had no time to take in the scenery. Chloe took the right, Randy the left. The young man ripped open the door and boldly thrust his head inside. It was a small room with a round table covered with two table clothes, one a red tapestry pattern that dropped to the floor and another smaller black cover that had tassels dangling from its edges. There were several fold up chairs set around the table and on one wall a very large metal sculpture of sun and moon profiles facing each other. No one was there. Meanwhile, Chloe sprinted into the candle room. She decided it was a significantly creepy place with burning candles everywhere and what looked like an altar or shrine against the long wall. At a glance she could make out two statues on the altar, one male with an antler headdress and the other a female in flowing Grecian robes holding a tall staff with crescent moons back to back. Spread out before the two figurines there was also bread, some grapes, apples and an ornate silver chalice encrusted with semi-precious stones and crystals. There were pictures on the wall directly above the altar and symbols and decorations she had never seen before. Gwen was nowhere to be found so Chloe turned tail and ran across the room they had just entered and prepared to bolt down the sunlit hallway with Randy who had just emerged from the smaller room. Both friends stopped dead in their tracks. At the far end of the hallway Gwen stood facing them expressionless. For a surreal few moments the three friends stared doe-eyed and dumbstruck.

Chloe was the first to shatter the silence.

"Are you alright!?"

Gwen's face sprouted a wide grin. "Sure. I'm fine. Why?"

"Where the Hell did you disappear to? You scared the crap out of Randy and me!!"

Chloe remembered the creepy lady might be barging through those drapes any second now. "Let's get out of here Gwen. You can tell us about it later."

Tarot cards are NOT just for foretelling the future. Here are several ways you can make good use of these beautiful decks that do not involve divination:

~Meditative tool

~Daily guidance

~Self-analysis

~Altar cards

~Energy & magick works

Your cards make use of symbolism and images that can have a powerful effect on the user. The axiom '*a picture is worth a thousand words"* is certainly true here. The pictures found in a typical deck relate to life experiences that are common to all of us. As I am fond of telling my own clients, nearly everyone passes through the stages and passages of life illustrated in the cards at some point. Who does not experiences loss, love and heartbreak, worry, success and defeat from time to time? A Tarot reading can serve several purposes simultaneously. It can tell you something about where you are now, that much is true, but it can also indicate your current trajectory and recommend possible alternate paths you might want to consider.

A good reading can pinpoint issues of particular importance to you at this particular juncture in your life. In my experience, they have an uncanny knack of zeroing in on what is important for you to pay attention to at any given moment, even if that was not what you came to the table asking about! It is common for people to ask about money, love or health only to have the cards warn of developing problems in their family life! They now have an opportunity to think about the issues that are being brought to their attention.

The Tarot can be a remarkable source of insight and help in navigating life's ever shifting seas. Having said that, there is reason for caution. Let us not forget that the cards can also be easily misinterpreted. This can happen for several reasons. Sometimes our own natural desire for a particular answer can skew our interpretation of the spread. Another cause of misreadings might be inexperience or a limited understanding of how the cards work. Furthermore, it is wise to be cautious about what the cards appear to say, even if the interpretation is correct. Why? Because the future is not written in stone but responds to what YOU do in the present. The present is your central point of power and influence. Today is always shaping tomorrow.

So, if readings are not 100% reliable and cannot be guaranteed to come true, why even bother with them? The answer is simple. It can offer clues, valuable tidbits of information and, sometimes, uncanny direction when other avenues of information are unavailable to you. Do we not tune in to the whether channel even if the forecast is not 100% reliable? A good reading can tell you what could happen IF you choose to continue down the path you're on now. In this way it can sometimes serve as an *early warning system* of sorts. While it is not recommended that you decide who to marry, which house to buy or if you should have children or not based on a Tarot reading, the cards can be consulted as PART of a rational and responsible decision making process. This process might include things like getting expert professional advice and doing your own research followed by a calm analysis of the facts. Tarot cards can be used to enhance and compliment your decision making process, but *never* as a substitute for thinking for yourself.

How Does it Work?

Some people believe that destiny rules every aspect of human life. Other people go to the opposite extreme and suggest that life is chaos and has no underlying rhyme or reason. These are philosophical questions that I will leave for others to debate. Likely the truth is somewhere in the middle. In my book there is unmistakable evidence that our world, functions according to natural laws. Laws like cause and effect, action and reaction, for example. For what it is worth, and with all due respect to the opinions of other people who might not agree with my next statement, it is my certain belief that EVERYTHING is connected to everything else on some level and as a result there is an underlying rhyme and reason to life. In my view, the many forces and energies that operate all around and within us can be understood and even influenced by individual humans, that is to say, US! You may not share this opinion, and that's OK but the reality of psychic phenomena, Tarot cards, Astrology and all the rest hangs on the concept that all things have an unseen commonality.

When you enlist the aid of Tarot cards you are asking the Universe to reveal some truth about your world in the spreads you draw from the deck. The Universe responds with images that have some bearing on your life. This may not make logical sense but anyone who has consulted the cards for any length of time will tell you that the cards often defy logic. As I am fond of telling people, logic has limitations and its conclusions are only as good as the information you put into the equation. The scientific community still does not know all the mysterious workings of our inner reality. Naturally, critics will dismiss this all with a chuckle but experience using the cards yourself will likely convince you that there is more at work here than meets the eye.

A Meditative Tool

One of the non-predictive uses of the Tarot is as a focal point for meditation. Select a card from the deck that inspires you or is a symbol of your desire. The cards cover most human wants and needs. For example, some appropriate cards might be the Lovers, the 10 of Disks, Ace of Wands, 6 of Disks, the Star, to name a few. Allow your mind to dwell on the image in all its parts and seek to understand on a deep personal level how it relates to you. The images can invigorate, inspire and strengthen you in nonverbal, spiritual ways if you ask them to.

Daily Guidance

You can do a daily drawing of 1 to 5 cards representing different aspects like body, mind, spirit, career, health, relationship, etc. The spreads can be can be used as a theme for the day. You can dwell on the spiritual thoughts engendered by the card (remember that even so-called 'negative' cards also have a positive aspect.) They can serve as warnings not to succumb to depression, defeat, melancholy or anger. You can also ASK the Tarot to indicate what your day will be like or what goals you should concentrate on this day.

Self-Analysis

This is a particularly helpful use of the archetypal imagery of the Tarot. Virtually every aspect of human strength and frailty is represented in these 78 cards along with a wide variety of personality types from emotional to intellectual to spiritual to mundane types. They can lead you to consult your intuition, draw from your inner energy sources or learn a new skill. By allowing your mind to dwell on the various cards, certain images, memories and emotions will surface in response to them. When this happens it is a great opportunity for you to ask yourself why you react the way you do. Be sure that you INTEND that particular spread be for self-analysis from the start. It is important that your question and intent be clear and to the point.

Altar Cards

This is yet another occasion where you can choose a card from the deck for a specific use as an altar tool. Some people like to use Tarot cards as altar cards because they are so rich in symbolism and meaning. In fact, those of us who use the cards frequently become very familiar with them and the symbols have become second nature to us, making them ideal for use on our altar space. Some cards can serve as focus points of protection, introspection, warning, strength and enlightenment. Feel free to use them on your altar as they are generally well suited to this purpose.

Magick and Energy Work

For the more adventurous of us the Tarot is also well suited for magickal use. They certainly can be used as a tool to focus our mental and emotional forces. Of course, as with the use of the cards for foretelling the future, some people may not feel comfortable with the whole concept of magick or spiritual manifestation. If magick is not your thing you may rest assured that Tarot cards were not originally designed for this particular purpose. As we have already demonstrated in this chapter, the cards are versatile and hold their value without resorting to their more mystical applications in magick or divination.

In a parting word about magick, suffice it to say that this is a subject that has generated wild exaggeration, fear and superstition fueled first and foremost by ignorance and misinformation. While it is well beyond the scope of this primer on Tarot reading to entertain this discussion, the simple truth is that labels misunderstood and misapplied can do as much harm as mislabeled prescription meds!

Chapter 5

Anatomy of a Tarot Deck

☙☙

"But I'm not done guys," Gwen objected. *"I can't leave now. It would be rude!"*

Randy was beside himself. "Oh YEAH, you ARE done girlie!! The old witch is gonna come back and we have to be gone. Now let's step while the steppin' is good!"

"That's fine." she said with a defiant upward swivel of her head. "You two can go. I'll catch up with you later."

Now it was Chloe's turn to be beside herself. "WHAT!!? What's wrong with you? Randy is right. We have to go NOW!" Her eyes began to search for another way out of this nightmare.

Gwen crossed her arms over her chest. "Listen. Mona is a nice lady. I don't know what your problem is. Why are you both so weirded out anyway? She doesn't bite ya know."

Just then Randy noticed the curtain held aside ever so slightly. They weren't alone anymore. The witch had been eavesdropping all the while!

⊱⊰

Modern Tarot card decks consist of 78 cards. They are divided into the Major and Minor Arcana. "Arcana" means *secrets* or *mysteries*. The Minor Arcana consists of 4 suits of 14 cards each. The Major Arcana contains 21 Trump cards and one Fool card. Cups, swords, wands, pentacles are the most common suits used today but the concept behind each suit remains more or less the same even if the names are different. For example, pentacles, disks, coins, cash, diamonds, gold all refer to the same characteristics that will be discussed later on.

What follows is a brief description of each of the suits and a small reference section wherein you can look up the generic, iconic meanings of each card. Please note that there are countless books on the Tarot in publication written by as many authors. Each book will couch the card meanings in somewhat different terms. Do not allow yourself to become confused or overwhelmed by all of this. Remember that when they were originally created there were no particular meanings attached to the cards that eventually developed into the Tarot we use today. Despite what any so-called authority might opine on the meanings and symbols on the cards, they are NOT written in stone. Decks don't even use the same symbols. They are, at best, traditional associations and interpretations that should be guidelines but never restraints to understanding the 'message' the cards have for you. This will allow you to develop a better internal rapport with each image and make it far easier to read the cards when you draw them. Do not imagine your intuitive perception and understanding of a given card is "wrong" simply because it doesn't jibe with the book description. The reading is a very personal thing and its interpretation is best left to the reader. I'm not suggesting you should make up just ANY interpretation of a card. It does have a specific interpretation but that will vary nearly every time you use it. The fact is it is more important what the card means to *you* than what a book says it does. For this reason the suggested meanings offered in this publication are brief and allow for personal interpretation.

There is a way of thinking about the suits that strikes me as a great way to explain the relationship they have to each other. The royalty cards and various characters in a deck can be viewed as individuals in a family setting. The suits describe the personality traits that their particular family share in common. Relating the card members to real people like you and me helps to understand them better.

All of us have met people whose personalities were characterized in large measure by the qualities related to the four Tarot suits. Take the suit of Cups, for example. Cups is the emotional suit. Feelings, sentiments, relationships, love (and hate) are all part of the mix here. The suit of Cups is where the heart and passionate drives live. An individual who is spontaneous, moody, affectionate, impulsive or hot-headed would definitely fit into a Cups personality. Therefore, the individuals depicted in the Cups suit will all have a significant emotional component. It will be easier for us to understand and remember what any individual in that suit is trying to convey to us if we are aware of his or her basic nature. If the individual in your reading is in the family of Swords we should remember that this is a calculating, pragmatic, practical more cerebral person. So it goes with the suits of Wands and Disks.

Suit characteristics and aspects

Swords:

This suit is all about the life of the mind. Logical evaluation, mental sharpness, cold calculation, pragmatic considerations, action, power.

Positive Aspects

Analytical
Authoritative
Discerning
Rational
Intellectual

Negative Aspects

Arrogant
Cutting
Cruel
Conflicting & confused
Destructive action

Cups:

This suit is where the heart and motivations live. Creativity, impulse, fantasy, love, rage, jealousy, loyalty, spontaniety, power, movement.

Positive Aspects

Love
Kindness & caring
Faithfulness & loyalty
Imagination
Action & movement

Negative Aspects

Rage
Obsession & fixation
Self-pity & hatred
Emotional repression
Listless and depressed

Suit characteristics and aspects

Wands:

Wands speaks to the true, inner, spiritual you. It lives at your core. Intuition, values, inspiration and creativity spring from this source.

Positive Aspects	Negative Aspects
Spirituality Inner strength Integrity & values Ambition Purpose & direction	Reckless Shallow Unproductive Egotistical Overwhelmed

Disks:

Disks are about mundane life. Money, health, family and the home. The practical issues of daily life, challenges and concerns.

Positive Aspects	Negative Aspects
Prosperity Health Manifestation Security Physical growth	Greed & envy Sickness & decline Materialistic & superficial Selfish, overindulgent Laziness & sloth

The Major Arcana

The Major Arcana are 22 cards in the deck that are called "Trump" cards. They are distinct from the rest and don't belong to the 4 suits. Remember that every card in your deck has BOTH positive and negative aspects and interpretations-even the more ominous looking ones. Even the "Death" card can have a positive message in a spread.

"0" ~ The Fool:

The Fool is a seeker, an adventurer who gives no heed to the criticisms of those who lack the courage to face the dangers of the unknown. "0" does not have the same limitations as other numbers. It is unquantified and therefore unemcumbered.

"1" ~ The Magician:

Also called the Juggler in some decks, this character has the potential to master life's various challenges with almost divine inspiration. This card speaks to one's talents and powers known and as yet undiscovered. The power of awareness and knowledge.

"2" ~ The Priestess:

Originally called the "Papessa," as in a female Pope, she can be a religious leader or a spiritual source of guidance. She personifies the subconscious mind, hidden wisdom and the gateway to higher knowledge and perception of occult truths.

The Major Arcana

"3" ~ The Empress:

She is the strong nurturing mother figure who both feeds and protects. Her embrace is loving but never forget she is also capable of "tough love." She is practical and has the wisdom to encourage earthly prosperity and good 'ole 'common sense.'

"4" ~ The Emperor:

The Emperor manifests as a confident, strong-willed and dominant individual who will always try to control and "rule" over things. While strong he (or she) may also be stubborn. There is power here but it must be tempered with compassion & kindness.

"5" ~ The Hierophant:

Also called the "Pope," this card links both heaven and earth. Wisdom, insight, compassion, law and mercy are symbolized. He can also be seen as a secular wise counselor, expert or adept. He is the one who brings divine wisdom to mundane problems.

"6" ~ The Lovers:

This card is not always about romance. It is about relationships and choices. Questions regarding balance, positive and negative interplay between 2 (or more) people can be at issue here. Also lessons on resolving conflicts & creating harmony from diversity.

The Major Arcana

"7" ~ The Chariot:

This card puts you in the drivers seat! It is BOTH about making choices and your capacity to move in the direction you decide. You must carry the full responsability for your choices and steer your mental and emotional "horses" to that end.

"8" ~ Adjustment:

Balance, judgment, justice, law are keys to understanding this one. It is good to examine different perspectives and see how so-called "opposites" can have much in common. Recall that life is about change and change usually requires adjustments. It's all good!

"9" ~ The Hermit:

The hermit is not a recluse. He/she is taking time for deep thought. This card prompts us to review our past, present and future for clues on how we can experience new growth. Even if we stand alone, there is a light that can illuminate our path.

"10" ~ Wheel of Fortune:

Often equated with good and bad luck, this card invites us to think seriously about how our own thoughts and actions bring either "good" or "bad" into our lives. The universe is orderly, not random, and there's more to life than the mere "luck of the draw."

The Major Arcana

"11" ~ Lust: (aka, Strength and Fortitude)

The "lust" spoken of here is not necessarily sexual. It is about passion and fire from deep within for some hotly desired goal. It motivates us to overcome fear and other obstacles to fulfill our dream, whatever that might be. It is genuine and profound.

"12" ~ The Hanged Man:

This card illustrates something we all experience occasionally. When life leaves us feeling 'bound up,' threatened, confused, frustrated and with few or no options, we feel like the Hanged Man. Remember, EVERYTHING changes in time. Keep hope alive!

"13" ~ Death:

This much feared card is not usually about death at all. It is what death symbolizes: profound, fundamental change, transformation, metamorphosis, endings and final completion. The ending of one "life" and the start of a new "life," path or journey.

"14" ~ Art: (aka, Temperance)

This is where we learn to combine disparate elements into something cohesive, harmonious and useful. Creative solutions win the day as we learn to balance what was not, learn to bring together things that don't appear to 'fit' and yet make it all work!

The Major Arcana

"15" ~ The Devil:

The Devil can symbolize malice, deceit, temptation or addiction. Negative human impulses imprison us. Medieval thinking faulted the Devil for the evil we humans should take responsibility for. This card reveals that we can escape our dilemma by owning it.

"16" ~ The Tower:

Sudden, unexpected, sometimes violent change is indicated. Although rarely welcomed this sort of change comes to us all and, more often than not, it precedes an opportunity to reconstruct and build a better situation in the aftermath. Keep centered & calm.

"17" ~ The Star:

'You are complete unto yourself.' You do not require another. Everyone has inner fortitude and self-worth. This card challenges us to see that truth. Unlock the storehouses of your talents and shine proudly for all to see. Avoid conceit but stand strong & tall.

"18" ~ The Moon:

The moon is a symbol of intuition, the subconscious and a reminder of female wisdom and power. Develop your intuition as it may help in making difficult choices. The moon reflects the sun but serves just as valuable a role. Both day and night have value.

The Major Arcana

"19" ~ The Sun:

Divine blessings, success, growth, power. Accepting the natural order of things aligns oneself with the powerful ebb and flow of Nature. 'Make hay' when the sun shines, change and adapt just as the seasons do, be grateful and accept full blessings everyday.

"20" ~ The Aeon: (aka, Judgment)

This is about the interplay of life cycles. Beginnings and endings, consequences, rewards, birth, life, death and resurrection. This card speaks to the many opportunities we have to remake ourselves, to evolve, learn from mistakes and make better choices.

"21" ~ The Universe:

The Universe is about balance and the harmony of opposites. This card places you at the center of the cosmos and all that is. It shows that we are part of a greater whole and comforts us with the knowledge that there is symmetry and reason behind it all.

I have intentionally avoided extensive explanations of the cards, astrological correspondences and symbol by symbol exposition. Why? The purpose of this workbook is to provide the tools you need to effectively read the Tarot for yourself and others. To use a simple analogy, I want to teach you the HOW-TO of driving a car, not give you a dissertation on auto mechanics! Sometimes *'less is more.'* I recommend you read a book written specifically for your deck. Finally, always keep learning via books, internet, classes, etc.

The Minor Arcana

This book is designed to smooth the path for people who want to use this oracle but who may also be somewhat intimidated by the high peaks of knowledge before them. It has been my experience that providing too steep a learning curve may discourage some students from starting to use what they learn at all! My advice; start slow and grow. What follows is a brief review of the Minor arcana.

Knight
- WANDS: Powerful, confident, fearless, fiery, rampant
- CUPS: Sensitive, sincere, intimate, vulnerable
- SWORDS: Focused, decisive, calculating, driven
- DISKS: Practical, realistic, hard working, responsible

Queen
- WANDS: Powerful, courageous, rebirth, forceful
- CUPS: Introspective, profound, intuitive, resourceful
- SWORDS: Insightful, mature, enlightened, clear sight
- DISKS: Authoritative, adventurous, strong, capable,

Prince
- WANDS: Fiery, powerful, ambition, potential
- CUPS: Changeable, refreshing, impulsive, deep
- SWORDS: Creative, ambitious, dynamic, progressive
- DISKS: Strong, stable, overseer of practical & earthly

Princess
- WANDS: Intense, impassioned, impetuous, brave
- CUPS: Reflective, resourceful, intuitive, receptive
- SWORDS: Resourceful, rigorous, skillful, pragmatic
- DISKS: Pioneer, developer, great potential, courage

Ace
- WANDS: Masculine, passion, fire, intention, power
- CUPS: Feminine, emotional, sincerity, power source
- SWORDS: Unification, insight, creative impulse
- DISKS: Materiality, rooted, gain, seeded growth

	Wands	Cups	Swords	Disks
Two	Bravery Courage Cooperation	Connection Partners Chemistry	Compromise Conflict Agreement	Transformation Intention Self-mastery
Three	Virtue Strength Integrity	Abundance Free-flowing Well-being	Realization Sorrow Heartbreak	Manifesting Relationships Accomplishment
Four	Completion New beginning Full circle	Overflowing Renewal Luxuriating	Meeting minds Truce Promise of peace	Stability Structure Boundaries
Five	Strife Silver lining Obstacles	Disappointment Discouragement Renaissance	Defeat Depression Illusion	Worry Beclouded Hope Enduring
Six	Victory Overcoming Obstacles	Pleasure Stronger & wiser Happy day	Well-made plan Allies & counsel Expertise	Success Well developed Tried & true
Seven	Valor Stand firm Inner strength	Disillusioned Putrefaction sickliness	Futility Adversaries Overwhelmed	Defeat Despair Depression
Eight	Options Choices Movement	Excess Plans failed Dysfunctional	Interference Distraction Dissenters	Prudence Protection Priorities
Nine	Strength Male/Female Keep Balanced	Happiness Harmony Fulfillment	Cruelty Criticism Bitter truth	Gain Harmony Stability
Ten	Oppression Restriction Tethered	Satisfaction Optimism Journey's end	Conflict Unrest Hurtfulness	Wealth Material whole Earth bound

Chapter 6

Worksheets

☙❦

"Hello dearies" Mona, aka 'the witch', said as she entered with just the hint of dramatic flair. Gwen, how nice. Who are your friends?

"Oh uhh.. well … we were just leaving ma'am." Randy managed a pitiful smile.

"Ah, hello! Hello! Maybe YOU were leaving but Mona and I were just beginning to get to know each other" Gwen chimed in imperiously.

It was obvious to Mona that the two youngsters were very uncomfortable. "Oh, that's too bad. Gwen, maybe we will talk another day. I'm open most days."

"Gwen said you came with questions. Have you changed your minds so quickly?"

Randy and Chloe exchanged uneasy glances but did not venture to speak.

Mona, noticed their hesitation and decided to see if she could salvage the situation.

"How rude of me! Let me introduce myself. My name is Mona. Welcome to my little corner of the world." She flashed that ingratiating smile and it seemed to shew away the tension that was hanging in the air.

☙❧

Learning the Tarot cards is a personal journey that is different for each individual. These worksheets can be an excellent start to learning the cards and, hopefully, at the same time a means to discover a bit more about yourself. To get the most from these pages be completely honest with yourself. Nothing can be gained by answering the questions in order to save face or protect a delicate ego. These answers are *for your eyes only*.

The symbolism of your deck may or may not be similar to other deck themes but that fact need not worry you. Do your cards employ Celtic runes, Numerology, Astrology or Egyptian iconography? They may not use symbols at all but rely mostly on a scene or image instead. It matters little that your deck is unlike other decks. What is important is that you 'make friends' with it, as it were.

What follows are worksheets that relate to alternative uses of the Tarot. Use them as thought starters. I hope they serve you well.

Fig. 5 Arthur Edward Waite (b. 1857-d. 1942) American born mystic, author, editor and co-creator of the famous Rider-Waite-Smith Tarot deck. Waite was a prolific author and penned books on divination, ceremonial magic, Kabbalism, Rosicrucianism, Freemasonry, Alchemy, etc.

Worksheet I: Meditative Tool

You can use any of the 22 Major Arcana or Trump cards as a launching point for a meditative journey. The images that have come down to us over the ages can be quite evocative. Pictures and symbols seem to be able to communicate directly with our subconscious minds. Becoming sensitive to the subtle reactions and emotions they evoke within can be valuable in gaining insight into our own inner workings.

Since we know every card has a positive and negative aspect, what positive or negative reactions does it inspire in you?

How do you express the two aspects of this card in your life?

What is your personal strength in relation to this card?

What is your personal weakness in relation to this card?

What about this card can make you a better, stronger person?

What ideas or thoughts cross your mind as you contemplate the image depicted on the card?

Do you find your attention drawn to one symbol or area? If yes, why do you feel that is so?

Is there any feature of this card that makes you feel uncomfortable, fearful, angry, discouraged, exhilarated, uplifted or any other strong emotion?

Do you have an affinity for this card or does it somehow reflect who you are?

Worksheet II: Daily Guidance

Daily guidance spreads can be drawn using from 1 to 5 cards in order to gain insight into either what sort of day you might have, if cards are chosen first thing in the morning, or what lessons the day taught you in hindsight, if the cards are cast in the evening. Some people consult the cards throughout the day as they feel the need. I would add a hint of caution here as it is entirely possible to become overly dependent on the cards, literally not being able to make a move without them! Keep your balance and use them sensibly. Never abdicate the rightful place thinking and fact finding have in making important decisions. Ask yourself the following questions:

What facet of your life does the spread appear to refer to?

How can you grow today? (grow as in smarter, wiser, stronger, in a word, BETTER)

Do you sense this spread is trying to warn you of something or give specific advice?

Will you do anything differently today as a result of this spread?

Do you get an emotional reaction to the spread? If yes, can you describe it?

Does it appear to have a positive or negative significance? Are there any actions you can take to improve things?

Do you feel the need to intentionally skew the interpretation of the spread to something more favorable?

Worksheet III: Self-Analysis

One of the best uses of the Tarot is as a tool to gain insight into oneself both present and past. Much has been said about the profound affect our childhood has had on who we are today. It is also true that many of us find the formative experiences of our youth near impossible to recall, to say nothing of sorting out the emotional issues they may have created. The cards may be of some help here as well.

You can intentionally question the Tarot regarding all aspects of who you are and who you were. The idea is to explore your emotional version of reality as you may perceive it. Do not forget that your own personal truth is just that, YOUR truth, your *version* of life. In other words, it is life according to YOU. The factual, objective truth of your life as seen by another person may be a rather different matter. Of course, it should go without saying that there is no substitute for consulting a trained mental health provider to help you deal with serious mental and emotional issues. Thankfully, in these modern times there is a growing awareness that people who avail themselves of psychologists and psychiatrists are no longer considered "crazy" or sick, simply intelligent enough to seek help when needed.

Notwithstanding the foregoing, however, you may be pleasantly surprised at the insights you gain from thoughtful introspection while using the cards as a springboard for exploring 'inner space.'

You may begin with 1 to 3 cards and ask about the important areas listed below. For this exercise you may either draw the cards randomly or search the deck and choose the card you prefer.

Look at the card and notice your own reaction to it. Where are your eyes drawn first? Do you know why?

Having taken inventory of your reactions to the card ask yourself *'what do these reactions say about me?'*

Worksheet IV: Altar Cards

The Tarot images illustrate the many passages of life. Love, loss, death, birth, sorrow, happiness, fear, courage and so much more are depicted symbolically in those 78 cards. It speaks to all aspects of what it means to be human. The spiritual, universal, magical and mundane realms are all included in a typical deck. Why is this useful? Because there is card for almost every situation where an altar might be used. Many people place a Tarot card or cards on an altar for any number of reasons. The word *altar* means to exalt or raise up. This *raising up* can be a spiritual thing or it can be exalting an idea or a desired goal. For example, if you are memorializing a beloved father who has passed you could use the Emperor or The Hermit. For instance, the Lovers card as well as the the Star can be used when a special someone is uppermost in your thoughts. Peruse your deck and you will see a card that could be ideal accessories for your Altar. Naturally, it is perfectly fine to use multiple cards since life is frequently a complex experience.

Altars vary widely in purpose and function. What will you use your altar for? Here are some ideas.

- ☐ Ancestral
- ☐ Memorial
- ☐ Celebration
- ☐ Healing
- ☐ Mood or meditation
- ☐ Shrine
- ☐ For working magick, energy working or spell casting

Once you decide the type of altar you want (you can have as many you like) consider the following questions.

Will you say a special phrase of blessing or make a special request of the card?

Are the symbols on the particular card you chose for your altar appropriate?

Worksheet V: Energy and Magick

Some people will have no use for this section. That is perfectly fine. The other non-magickal applications for Tarot are still worth your time. Remember that the cards were never designed with magick in mind. As noted earlier, the Tarot began as ordinary decorative playing cards made for people who could afford to have them painted by artists. In time they were also used for divination but the same could be said of commonplace cards used to play Poker, Pinocle or Gin.

Magick in theory and practice is not the subject of this workbook, so I will touch on the role of Tarot cards as a magickians tool as lightly as possibly while still providing some context. After all, a discussion of the cards would hardly be complete without, at least, alluding to this application. If you are interested in learning real magick craft there are many sources of information and guidance, myself included.

The magick worker should both ask and answer the following questions of him or herself.

Have the cards been ritually cleansed or made "neutral" for this working?

Have they been enchanted to the specific purpose desired?

If there are symbols on them, do you understand those symbols and are they in harmony with the working?

Has the goal of your working been stated clearly and completely?

Have you determined the card is aligned with the appropriate correspondences such as gender, astrology, elements, magickal timing, moon phases, deities (if any), colors, etc.?

Of course, no card will correspond in every way to your purpose but they are powerful in the right hands!

Chapter 7

"Spreads" to Suit Your Needs

ಶಿಲ್ಡ

Mona continued, "Now, what is all this about questions? Who will be first?"

Chloe perked up. "We are doing a school report on fortunetelling and Tarot cards. We can get extra credit if we can interview somebody who uses them."

"I see" the old lady began. "OK then. Now we're getting somewhere. What exactly do you want to know?

Randy, the most skeptical of the three, jumped right. "How can cards tell the future? They're just cards." "Are they SPECIAL cards?" He said that last bit smiling broadly and waggling his fingers up by his face as though he was conjuring something "witchy" and amazing!

"Do you know magick!?" Chloe erupted. Clearly the initial ill-placed fear had past. Instead the youngsters were now full of

curiosity and bursting with questions. Mona quickly determined that this little educational session could take more time than she might have to spare. But she had an idea.

Oddly enough, Gwen had no questions. She remained quiet. Mona looked at her with a knowing gaze. There was warmth and compassion in the old woman's eyes. It wasn't that Gwen had no questions, it was that she had too many. Something about this place affected her deeply. It wasn't the sunset orange-yellow color of the walls or the dried grapevines that adorned the ceilings. It wasn't the flickering candlelight that seemed to make every shadow a living thing. She didn't know why but it was like she has found something long lost. Not only was it lost but even its memory was lost. This special 'something' was somehow within reach and now Gwen had the most curious feeling that she was exactly where she was always meant to be.

ஐௐ

Spreads are one of the devices invented long ago to impose a certain structure or method on a reading. Typically the cards are laid out in patterns that can take many forms. The position of each card in the spread is assigned a particular focus or area of life. The card you draw that gets placed in that spot in the pattern may be read as it pertains to career or family or family, your present or past, for example. Using spreads definitely has advantages. I suggest you experiment with and without the benefit of a preassigned spread and see what feels comfortable. While structure makes some people feel more secure it has the opposite affect on other individuals.

Some spreads, like the Celtic Cross spread, for example, speak to your whole life. A smaller pattern may have a more limited focus. You will see what I mean when you review the spreads I have collected in this chapter. You should know that you are perfectly capable of creating your own spreads to suit your needs. There is nothing mystical or hard about doing this. There are no secret formulas or hard and fast rules here. You will see that the main idea is to create a spread that covers the issues you are inquiring about. Each position in your pattern will be assigned a 'post' or topic it is being asked about. When you lay out the cards the one that lands in position "1" will be interpreted as it relates to 'careers' or 'health' or whatever topic is assigned to that position. It is no difficult task to design your own spread if you give it just a bit of thought. As a for instance, if you are are drawing a simple daily spread you might choose to ask what will be your lessons or challenges this day in the following three areas: spiritual, physical, emotional. You would only have to decide if the cards will be lined up in a row with the card in left position being designated as 'spiritual,' middle 'physical,' and right mental/emotional self, for example. Or you might prefer to lay them out in triangular pattern, indicating that one of those areas is a pinnacle issue for you. It is rather simple really and requires no exceptional spiritual gift. The main thing is to be consistent. It is better to use whatever spreads you like often enough to become familiar with them.

Let us consider one last point before going on to the various spread patterns. There are spreads formed to represent crowns, crescents, pentagrams, castles, etc., etc. There are probably dozens of them. This book includes only a handful of these patterns. Why not include more? Because if you read the text that goes along with each spread you will notice that they repeat themselves. There are only a few variations on the theme. Most every spread will have a designated spot for the past, present and future, a challenge or obstacle card and so on. You will begin to see that in most cases the pattern you lay the cards out in doesn't really matter since most spreads will speak to the same, or at very least, similar issues. In my experience the true difference in any given reading are the questions that are put to the cards and not whether the pattern is shaped like a tree of life, a Chakra column or a crescent moon. As always I recommend you experiment to discover what works best for you.

The Celtic Cross Spread

This is one of the most widely used spreads, especially when doing a 'whole life' reading on someone for the first time. You will see that it covers most bases in the average person's life. One last point before we go on. Although there is only one card assigned to each position in a spread you are free to delve more deeply into a particular area in the following ways: you can draw additional cards to that one topic. It is as if you are asking the cards to expand its explanation in that one area. You can do this by drawing from the remaining cards that are not already part of the spread. Another method would be to collect all the cards back into the deck and re-shuffle them. When your querant is shuffling they should be thinking about the question asked.

Some spreads have a card marked "S." This is called the Significator. The Significator is usually a character or 'face' card and should reflect the querent's personality as its presence in the spread is supposed to represent him or her. Beginning with the Significator as the very first card selected you should then deal the remaining cards out in the order they are numbered. Preferably he/she should choose this card for themselves, but this may not be practical or possible for any number of reasons. In that case either choose one on their behalf based on your sense of who they really are at their core or, as an alternative, simply decide this card will be read as a comment on the situation overall.

1. The Crossing Card: What the querent may need to see/understand.

2. The Foundation: the core issue, the pivotal thing, the key factors.

3. The Near Future: Not a prediction but rather a potential outcome.

4. The Crown: the goal, the desire, the thing hoped for.

5. Recent past: what leads up to or contributes to the situation.

6. The querent: this comments on his/her feelings or place in it.

7. The Surroundings: people that have input/influence into the situation. Do they help or hinder?

8. Hopes and Fears: this card helps the querent sort out their feelings.

9. The final outcome: The Tarot is great for revealing what I call a "future trajectory." In other words, if all things continue as they are, this particular thing will happen in the future. In other words, your actions today are constantly creating and altering your future trajectory

Frieda Harris, aka, "Lady" Frieda Harris (b. 1877- d. 1962) was an artist who is known today primarily for her work on the Thoth Tarot deck. Although most credit goes to Aliester Crowley for creating this exceptional deck, it was Harris who encouraged him to go well beyond his original intent which was to create a conventional Tarot set. Crowley himself characterized her contributions as "genius."

The Chakra Spread

This "spread" is simply a vertical column of 7 cards starting with #1 at the bottom (closest to you) and ascending to #7 at the top.

Chakras are energy centers or turning energy "wheels" that are part of your auric or astral body. The balance or imbalance of these centers may affect your physical, mental and emotional health. While contemplating the seven major Chakras located in your torso from the base of the spine to the crown of your head you may focus on the lessons contained in preselected cards as they relate to each Chakra. There are no hard and fast rules about how one should analyze the cards in this spread. You do well to learn about the main Chakras in order to understand the relationship between a card and the energy center in question.

7. Crown
6. Third eye
5. Throat
4. Heart
3. Solar Plexus

2. Sexual center

1. Root

The Crescent Spread

1. Past: how past events affect the present or the question posed.

2. Present: what the current situation is/what you need to see.

3. Future: what the future brings, what is developing.

4. What's on the querent's mind: helps to analyze the querent's thoughts/feelings.

5. Attitudes of others: note: you can request specific individuals views.

6. Challenge: this is an obstacle or challenge that must be overcome.

7. Outcome: This is what could happen.

The Tree of Life Spread

Significator (S): See the Celtic Cross spread.

1. Aims or ideals: This is what the querant wants, the goal, objective.

2. Influences: Can be people, circumstances or your own issues.

3. General description: This is the core issue being addressed.

4. key: This is an important factor that might be overlooked.

5. Influences of the Present: Take these things into account.

6. Influences of the Future: this is more or less self explanatory.

7. Effect of the Significator: this is his/her own part in the matter.

8. Effect of the Environment: includes everything around the issue

9. Hopes and Fears: the querant's own hopes and fears.

The Final Outcome: where the situation is leading to.

The General Spread ~ 3 cards

I've used this spread many times myself. In the 3 card version the positions can correspond to either mind, body, spirit or past, present and future. Since this particular spread is not intended for a comprehensive whole life reading it is ideal for a bit of insight from day to day.

The General Spread ~ 9 cards

This pattern is versatile and can either be adapted for a daily spread or a whole life reading. Personally I use it for virtually every sort of reading. Hopefully, it has become clear by now that the reader has wide latitude in deciding how a spread can be interpreted. For example, the top row of 3 cards can be read as past, the middle 3 as present and bottom 3 as future. The 3 cards on each level can either be assigned a "post" of your choosing, in other words, family, personal and public relations, for example or you may borrow bits and pieces from another spread if you wish.

Spiral Dance Spread

The Spiral Dance can serve as a whole life spread as well as a more in depth study into a particular situation you may be creating intentionally or manifesting inadvertently.

Cards 1 through 3 represent the past leading up to the present. The upper left hand set of 3 cards, 15, 11 and 7 speak to the future or potential that is available to you. Cards 4, 8 and 12 in the upper right hand corner illustrate the sort of future you are creating currently. The lower right hand corner have cards 5, 9 and 13 describe the future outcome that is in store for you. Finally, the 3 cards in the lower left of the spread, 14, 10 and 6 reveal your challenges, obstacles but also your allies and resources. If you lay out the cards in order starting with #1 you will be following a spiral path. You do not necessarily need to read them that way but this spread carries the idea that life is a process of unfolding and growth. Whether we realize it or not we are at the center of our lives participating in the creation of our tomorrows today.

Chapter 8

Symbolism and Correspondences

☙CB

Now this kindly old lady, formerly known as 'the witch' clasped her hands together and leaned slightly forward. With a twinkle in her eye she spoke.

"I have an idea dearies. They say a picture is worth a thousand words. So how many words are 78 pictures worth? What say I SHOW you the answers to your questions? I will cast the Tarot for one of you and the other two can take notes. Fair enough?"

Chloe looked a bit sheepish. "The thing is... we don't have any money."

"Who said anything about money? Your money is no good here. It's the least I could do for three brave souls who risked life and limb to visit 'the witch!" With that Mona let fly a loud, raucous laugh that left the three youths unsmiling and all wondering the same thing; 'was she putting us on or was that a REAL witch's cackle?'

☙CB

One of the most interesting features of the modern Tarot is the variety of symbols, imagery and cultural diversity expressed in it. This, however, is a two edged sword, as they say. These elements are helpful to experienced persons on the one hand but it can be a little intimidating for the novice. As I have suggested earlier, do not shrink back from using the cards because you are not an expert reader yet. Do not forget that they will still be useful even at the level of your current understanding. Having said that, you should also be aware that your knowledge and understanding have limits (and always will,) so it is wise to give your counsel with humility and in the spirit of a seeker after truth. Do not comport yourself as the 'all knowing' seer or dogmatically insist your interpretation is flawless.

There are millions of religious and spiritual symbols that have been devised throughout human history in thousands of cultures worldwide. Most of us are only aware of a tiny fraction of them at best. Although the modern deck has a standard structure and common meanings the very wide variety of themes, artists interpretations and symbols, however, can and do significantly impact the messages conveyed. For this reason a Tarot book that is created for your specific deck can be helpful. If no book is available it really shouldn't stop you from becoming a good reader.

Since the whole reading process is a personal and subjective one you do well to develop the ability to sense what "feels right." As with most things, you get out what you put in.

The most common symbols on modern decks are Egyptian, Numerological, astrological, Hermetic, Celtic, Kabalistic and those based on the mystical tradition of the Golden Dawn. Needless to say, there are many others. If your deck has nsymbols learn them. You will find that certain cultures, symbolism and pantheons have a special appeal to you. Follow your gut and try out a deck that calls to you.

Here's something to keep in mind. Your interpretation of any given card will not usually include all the features on it. Every reading you do, even if you only read yourself, will be different. Sometimes the "message" or reading of a card will be *different* for one person than another! When you turn over a card and first set eyes upon it, ask yourself, *"what did I notice first?"* What impression or thought occurred to you in that moment? Did your eye alight upon a symbol or a specific feature in the picture? Was it the color that jumped out at you or was it a crow perched on a tree limb? These first flashes are often intuition trying to draw your attention to a pertinent feature in the card as it applies to the situation at hand.

If you are like most people, before you even have a chance to hear that quiet "little voice" of intuition, the rational mind jumps in to take over the show and begins to process the experience logically. At this point your subtle, fleeting impressions usually get drowned out and the quality of the reading takes a nose dive. The degree to which you learn to pay attention to that quiet, inner voice, will determine how accurate and ultimately helpful, your Tarot consultation will be. Honestly, after having taught seminars on reading Tarot I can tell you that most people are too nervous or so fixated on doing it "right" they aren't able to hear that soft intuitive voice. No worries. If you use the cards frequently you will reach a level of comfort that will allow you to relax and focus on the impressions from an intuitive place.

Be patient! Don't be discouraged if you find yourself with the book clutched in hand, looking up each card's meaning in your spread. Almost EVERYONE started out that way, including me! If you don't hear that intuition whisper in your ear right away, don't fret. Simply learn the cards at your own pace. Have fun with it and don't take yourself too seriously. You need time to become comfortable with your cards.

Common Symbols and what they mean:

Angel	Messenger, servant, herald, righteousness
Ankh	Life, immortality, union of male/female
Armor	Protection, preparation, battle, threat
Bird	Air element, spirit, far-sightedness, loftiness
Bridge	Passages, change, a way out, choices to make
Bull	Power, stability, virility, stubborn, force
Butterfly	Transformation, renewal, progress, beauty
Caduceus	Healing, balance, spiritual power, duality
Cat	Stealth, awareness, occult, cautious, seeing
Chains	Bondage, unhappiness, self-imprisonment
Children	Potential, innocence, hope, beginnings
Circles/Balls	Wholeness, worlds, understanding, infinity
Clouds	Heaven, hidden mystery, lack of clarity
Dog	Loyalty, honesty, humility, truth, friendship

Dove	Purity, love, blessing, Spirit/God, chosen one
Falcon	Clear vision, loftiness, superiority, powerful
Fire	Purification, destruction, passion, energy
Fish	Emotion, intuition, subconscious, abundance
Flag	Announcement, pride, change, unity, action
Flower	Beauty, growth, Nature, romance, joy, love
Grapes	Fertility, luxury, youth, pleasure, hospitality
Hand	Power, authority, instruction, give & take
Heart	Love, desire, passion, sincerity, strength
Horns/music	Pronouncement, victory, heavenly, signaling
Horns/antlers	Strength, sovereignty, courage, exploration
Horse	Strength, vitality, dignity, travel, nobility
Keys	Freedom, solutions, knowledge, authority
Lantern	Insight, understanding, guidance, goodness
Lemniscate	Infinity, endlessness, god, timelessness, Spirit
Lion	Power, royalty, danger, destroyer, animalistic
Mountains	Challenge, lofty goals, obstacle, achievement
Ocean	Profound wisdom, power, Self, rise/fall of life
Path	Choices, beginnings/endings, travel, career

Ram	Determination, leadership, authority, power
River/falls	Eternal, emotions, subconscious, boundaries
Scales	Balance, judgment, accounting, justice
Scroll/book	Knowledge, learning, secrets, wisdom
Shield	Protection, vigilance, caution, vulnerability
Ship	Journey, passages, transformation, death
Snake	Renewal, rebirth, wisdom, caution, flexibility
Sphinx	Guardian, life mysteries/secrets, synergy
Staff/rod	Authority, self-determination, quest, support
Star	Guidance, illumination, inspiration, wishes
Sun	Divine blessing, god/goddess, revelation
Sunflower	Look to the light, divine direction, positivity
Wall	Obstacle, separator, defenses, prison, shelter
Wolf	Primal instinct, spirit led, loyalty, wisdom

Chapter 9

Numbers and What They Mean

※

"I'm alone to run the store right now," Mona explained, "but my helper, Stella, comes by to help me after school. She'll be here in about fifteen minutes. Why don't you look around the store for a bit and when she arrives we can all go to the reading room. What say you kiddies?"

Chloe and Randy huddled together in the store, going over their list of questions and mumbling a little nothing about everything. Gwen spent the time exploring every nook and cranny of this magickal place.

Mona finished lighting the last of many candles and all three youngsters were struck with the natural beauty of this tiny sanctuary. Gwen sensed that nature was in balance here. Suddenly she was jealous of Stella, a girl her age whose job allowed her to bask in the healing energies of this secret sanctuary.

"So then, who shall it be? Which one of you will take the plunge?

Not surprisingly, Gwen was fairly bursting with anticipation. Mona knew this but intentionally passed her over. "Randy, would you care to be the chosen one?" Mona said with a knowing smirk. Being a skeptic, he was the perfect candidate.

"Sure. No problem" he answered, feigning confidence he did not feel. Taking the seat opposite Mona they were finally ready to begin.

Mona took hold of her lighter and lovingly lit the candle on the table itself. She mumbled something under her breath and explained that the candle flame was a symbol of the spirit of God that enlightens everyone who draws near to it. She began to shuffle the deck and did so for some few minutes. She then handed it to Randy and then gave a nod. It was his turn to touch the cards.

꙰

Numbers feature prominently in the Tarot. Fortunately there is much information available about Numerology and Sacred Geometry. The meanings associated with each number are more consistent and not as open to interpretation as pictographs and symbols are. Why not try reading using only the numbers? You may actually feel very comfortable consulting the cards in this way. This is what readers do with standard playing cards. The only references they have are the numbers, the suits and the royalty cards. Using Tarot cards in this way is entirely appropriate and will serve you well if you are comfortable with this method.

Number Associations:

Zero: Beginning and ending, Alpha and Omega, limitless, infinite, unity, infinite potential.

One: Independence, action, motivation, singleness of purpose, drive, positivity, will, power, unity.

Two: Balance, contrast, opposites, partnership, communication, negotiation, choice.

Three: Time, divinity, creativity, strength, versatility, mystery, intuition, family, advancement.

Four: Stability, endurance, practicality, physicality, balance,

Five: Motion, travel, adventure, passion, humanity, unpredictability.

Six: Sincerity, unfolding, protection, sensitivity, dependability, growth, nurturing.

Seven: Spiritual perfection, imagination, awareness, mysticism, understanding, healing.

Eight: Business, opportunity, intention, abundance, pragmatic, infinity, organization.

Nine: Vision, invention, attainment, anticipation, completion.

Aliester Crowley (Edward Alexander Crowley) (b. 1875- d. 1947.) Both famous and infamous but undeniably significant, Aliester Crowley was an occultist, ceremonial magickian, British secret agent, author, mountaineer, poet and founder of the religion and philosophy of Thelema.

Chapter 10

So What Now?

ಜ∞ಣ

The three youngsters felt a collective pit in their tummies as Randy placed the now shuffled deck on the table. The moment was finally here. Randy's eyes were locked on the deck as if it was a roadside bomb that might explode any second now. Mona could feel his anxiety, not to mention seeing his hands clenched one to the other as if holding on for dear life!

"Relax, son. Nothing bad will happen here. The cards are here to help you. Always to help." Randy's lip twitched into a half-smile. Then his eyes darted back to the bomb on the table.

Mona turned over the first card, then the second, the third and finally dealt out ten cards into the traditional Celtic Cross spread. She took a few moments to survey the spread as they spoke to the various areas of life and also past and future. There was no rush to speak.

She began; "This card is called the Significator. It is all about you here and now. What you deal with and what is happening in your life currently. You drew the Princess of Swords young man." Mona *smiled widely and continued. "You see the girl on this card is swinging her sword all around through the clouds and smoke?"*

Randy's brow furrowed up in confusion. "But that's a girl and I'm a boy!"

"Yes, I know sweetie. It is no matter. It is what she is doing that is important. Like you her mind is quick and wants to do many things in her life. She's ambitious. Her problem is that she needs to learn that not everything can be understood by just being smart. Do you notice how she is leaning back onto that altar or pile of bricks?"

Mona picked up the card and turned it so Randy could see it clearly what she was talking about.

"Well, sometimes she can bite off more than she can chew. Do you know what that expression means?" She watched for an affirmative nod. "Look at what is happening to you today, son. Your mind is exploring a new world. There is so much you have seen today that you do not understand. The swords are symbols of your thoughts. It is the world of the mind this card refers to. You are a thinking person who likes things to make logical sense. Randy you are a little taken aback, just like the person in the card. You are temporarily off balance. Does this make sense to you? This is an opportunity for you to grow, Randy. Try to see that there is a much bigger world out

there than logic knows about- yet!"

"Yeah... I guess. Gwen always says that even geniuses don't know everything."

ఴఌ

You have the basics at your fingertips. What are you waiting for? The key to using the cards effectively is USING them. Do not hesitate to ask them questions frequently, even everyday. Tarot is not well suited to yes-no questions, but it can comment on virtually every facet of your life. Some people carry a deck with them everywhere for quickie consultations as the need arises. There are miniature decks that fit handily into a pocket or purse.

Without becoming dependent on the cards to make decisions for you, practice interpreting the cards intuitively, with no fuss or fret. Remain relaxed and calm. Get to the point where you do not need to consult a book for the definitions of each card.

How to do a reading in 5 easy steps

1- Decide what question or knowledge you desire from the Tarot. If you are religious, have a saint, deity or spirit guide you trust, ask for their assistance to make the proper interpretation. If you are not religious that also is fine, simply be specific in your question.

2- Shuffle the deck thoroughly. There is no wrong way to do this so long as it is thoroughly remixed since last use.

3- Use whatever spread suits your question best. Draw the cards from the top of the shuffled deck and lay them out.

4- Look at each card in turn with a fresh and open mind. What are the first thoughts that come to you? How do they relate to the spread position and your question? Don't prejudge or intellectualize too much. Recall that the intuitive interpretation of even the same card can vary with each reading. If your intuition still needs tweaking consult your book.

5- Consider the cards even if they don't seem to make much sense just now. If an interpretation doesn't come to mind, don't fret. Don't push the process. Sometimes I write down the cards and their positions on paper so I can revisit them later. And don't forget that sometimes not knowing what's next is best. Some life lessons can only be learned the good old fashion way, first hand and without forewarning! Knowing what will happen ahead of time is not always a good thing.

Finally, at the risk of having a reader exclaim, "oh God, not THIS again!!" one point bears repeating. While the Tarot is a wonderful tool, never allow it to cripple your ability to make important decisions without "mystical" help. I have had clients became so dependent on readings they could hardly decide what color shoes to wear without consulting me! One such client left me no choice but to end our professional relationship. Hopefully, this also ended her unhealthy dependency. Here's a word to the wise. Beware of any professional reader that is willing to feed an addiction to readings, gradually milking your wallet dry. These unscrupulous individuals will keep the unwary customers coming back forever without ever really helping them to solve their problems. Our goal as readers should be to HELP clients, not turn them into human cash dispensers!

So what now? Hopefully you are now fully aware that the Tarot is far more than a tool for divination and fortunetelling. It has many uses that can be employed everyday. Whatever your particular interest in Tarot do not forget that while the future can sometimes be divined with some accuracy, foreknowledge is not necessary to live a full and happy life. In some way *not knowing* what tomorrow brings is a *good* thing. How so? Getting stronger, smarter, better prepared for an unknown tomorrow causes us to evolve and develop. The fact that we don't know what tomorrow will bring can move us to cherish each day and the special people in our lives. Life is not intended to be lived as a 'rerun' of something already foreseen. To the contrary, the keen anticipation of what will happen next is what makes life so special. Not even the most gifted psychics can know the future with precise certainty. Why not think of the cards as a group of friendly advisers that offer their counsel and lay out possible future scenarios for you to consider? Follow that up with applying your best judgment to the matter. Remember, facts are your friends and intuition is your friend. Using that two-handed, right and left brained approach to coping with life's challenges is a sure way to tap your full potential.

Duke and Duchess of Bavaria. Inscribed with the date 1500. From Singer 1816.

Chapter 11

The End... or the Beginning?

Mona proceeded to the card in the number 1 position.

"This card tells us what challenges you, Randy. The card drawn for you is the 9 of Disks. In my deck this is called 'Gain.' Since it is the suit of Disks it refers to material or mundane issues. Material gain is a great thing if we are talking about money or home life. But since this card is in the challenge position it tells us that this is a problem you need to give attention to. Since you are a thinking person who is ambitious, it seems to say you may possibly be neglecting important issues on the home or family front. How are things at home Randy?"

Randy hung his head. He didn't know what to say. The truth was only last week his mom and dad had a pow-wow with him about not spending enough time at home. He couldn't understand what the big deal was. He just liked hanging with his geeky friends and doing geeky things. He figured his parents should be happy he was using his brain and spending time with smart kids instead of doing drugs or gang banging. He had to admit home life wasn't really on his priority list. Maybe mom and dad weren't being totally ridiculous after all!

All randy could do was say, *"Everything's OK, I guess."* Mona was sensitive to the fact that friends were listening in on the reading and Maybe Randy might not want to discuss it in front of them. Instead she decided not to press the issue and simply moved on to the next card.

The reader proceeded through the rest of this whole life spread, looking for lessons to relate and giving helpful insight wherever her intuition and the cards indicated. Randy had many new things to think about that day. He also gained a new respect for Mona and the uncanny accuracy of the reading. He still couldn't wrap his head around how it was possible to get so much out of a random selection of cards but, he also couldn't argue with the insight Mona seemed to have into his private life, the life of someone she had never met before.

The youths lingered in the store as Mona tended to various chores. By then the shadows had grown long and they were about to depart when Chloe's cell phone rang. It was a sign that the time had come to return to the outside world. It was her mom inviting Randy and Gwen to dinner and a movie. Randy thought for a long moment and then declined. "Sorry Chloe, I think I'm gonna surprise mom and have dinner at home tonight." He couldn't explain why but, something deep inside him just felt 'right.'

Notes:

www.ingramcontent.com/pod-product-compliance
Lightning Source LLC
Chambersburg PA
CBHW042016150426
43197CB00002B/43